The Story So Far

The Story So Far

David Allen

Writers Ink Press
Long Island, New York

2004—2008

For Ruth Ellen,
my muse
the love of my lives

ACKNOWLEDGEMENTS

Thanks to the following publications in which poems have appeared: The Ryukyu Shimpo, Shi, Old Friends, Unitarian Universalist News Net, the Eat Write Café, Poetry Today Online, Sentinel Poetry.

PREFACE

Poets are allowed to make lists to tell us their "Story So Far," as long as it's an interesting list. David Allen's is and thus, so are his poems—a good life that makes a good read. American poets, in other countries, are sometimes chided for taking even little details from their lives and turning them into poetry. That's a large part of the art that David Allen has mastered—solidly, happily in the American tradition.

Allen is not averse to autobiography, not needing that mask of fiction behind which so many artists hide. Of course that is true in his title poem which catalogs his personal journey. It is most poignant in poems such as "Requiem for My Father," which recites a litany of pain and in so doing purges the past, leaving a "demon-less Dad." He writes to atone for the fact that "I Never Wrote a Poem About My Mother," creating a poem even more powerful because it celebrates a life that was so often bullied into a position of powerlessness.

Allen's poems are a often a plain song in performance of a homey philosophy. For those who search for god, "In the Country" asks "if god/ is afraid of the dark." In "No Sense," we contemplate a god who "is either/ absent minded,/ a practical joker,/ or a sadist." His "Meaning" is something you can "put...in your pocket...go off whistling/ down the street."

"Anticipation," delights us with music "like a cool chill on a steaming/ day of city summer stranger streets." "Nightmares," turns philosophy into a song, something

Allen may have learned from his father who "plays the mandolin/ when life begins to close him in." Allen even has moments one could liken to Emily Dickinson, as in "Underneath."

The Pulitzer-prize-winning poet Louis Simpson, himself inclined to cataloging the oddities of "American Poetry," has also noted that many poets seem to want to be novelists. Allen himself, in "The Final Chapter," promises "No more novel, play or poem similes." Luckily, he contradicts this pronouncement many times in this book. His relaxed lines and narrative tendencies might remind you of "novel." In truth, he has a professional journalist's talent for writing good lead lines, a poet's ear for music and the strong endings of a story writer. Blending forms, he is a poet who more than gives us— he gifts us his life in poetry!

He explains his modus operandi in "Running" noting how writing has been his refuge and salvation even as "book walls crumbled/ and, crippled, I learned to crawl." Indeed, he's gone much further than that humble admission in the Story So Far. He puts a well-earned, positive slant on his accomplishments in "Seesaw Sensations," exclaiming "Ah, so this is living." Hooray for David Allen's courage, creativity and poetry!

David B. Axelrod, Fulbright Poet
www.poetrydoctor.org

CONTENTS

Tain't Nothing

"This writing's not all
that hard," he said,
peering over the poet's shoulder.
"After all, you never
even learned
to type,
and look how
well you do."

(But he never saw the callused pads
of my type-dancing shoes.)

The Story So Far

Over 50,
Damn!
Now I've done it;
gone full blown
into the middle of
my sixth decade.
Weird to think the toes
that toddled into the second half
of this century
are stubbing themselves
on the doorstep
of the new millennium.

Like the Grateful Dead
liked to sing:
"What a long, strange
trip it's been."

A child of the South,
raised in the North,
because my Yankee Dad
fell in love with television.
Grew up on Long Island
when there was still room
for clammers, before you could
walk across the harbor on the decks
of the boats of the rich.

Traveled a lot–
Lived in the Southeast,
the Mid-Atlantic,
Virginia mountains and shore,
D.C., Williamsburg,
Fort Wayne, Indiana—
dubbed that cold city the
"Crack Capital of the Midwest."

Lots of traveling
through two marriages,
five kids and four dogs;
finally getting it right
on the subtropical shores
of Okinawa.

Caught the news Jones
as a kid peddling papers.
Made it a living after trying out
being a busboy, dishwasher, cook,
sailor, postal worker, pump jockey,
shipping clerk, disc jockey,
student, activist, cabby,
surveyor.

Finally found work
on a weekly;
rhyming beat,
sports and courts,
at $120 a week.
Caught that news Jones bad,
still need that daily fix

only a byline gives.
Thirty years on deadline,
almost half a life;
printer's ink for blood;
thick skin, thin wallet.
Press cards, a passport
to the adrenaline rush
a good story brings.

Writing just felt right.
Still does.

Fifty-plus years—
where'd they go?
Playing war with sticks and clods of mud;
protesting war with shouts, upraised fists;
Washington demonstrations and
Central Park Love-Ins;
Nights at the Fillmore East,
some new band called Led Zeppelin
playing to half a house;
Woodstock, bluegrass festivals;
experiments with hallucinogens and booze
about as carelessly considered
as choosing eggs or cereal
for breakfast.

Fifty-plus years—
always observing, writing;
boxes full of unfinished journals,
jotted thoughts that somehow found their way into
stories, poems, letters.

Started *Old Friends*, a slip into
publishing, providing poets
and photographers a place
to lay it all out;
great idea at a bad time
for cash-poor gypsies.
Scattered poems published since
until running into the Eat Write folks.
This feels good,
think I'll hang out a while.

Fifty-plus years—
seen a lot;
murder, mayhem, floods and fires,
twisters tearing up trailers,
typhoons triumphant,
earthquake rocking the house:
boys laughing, what a ride!
girls crying, what a horror!
Seen the bare-breasted women of Yap,
Hoosiers bundled, braving a wintry blast;
the hookers and whores of San Juan,
Manila and all ports in between;
saw Sodom and Gomorra in
a Thailand town called Pattaya;
ate political chicken dinners,
drank iced rum milk from a chilled coconut;
saw Santa drop sleds of Christmas cheer
parachuting from the rear of an old cargo plane
as the natives of Palau sang Christmas carols
in their native tongue.

Fifty-plus years—
saw love come and go,
knocking at my door
and running away.
Saw hunger, but not lately.
Saw poverty, but that's past.
Had health and heartache;
still cry easily.
Saw a mother torn from her daughter
and sit on the floor tearing Bibles.
Saw the bodies of little girls,
naked, mutilated,
torn from life and left for dead
in some rain swollen ditch.
Saw a woman go insane.

Fifty-plus years—
saw a lot of smiles,
heard much hearty laughter.
wrote my own wedding
once I found my soul mate;
didn't matter she gave me only two years,
I knew we'd be together forever.
We still are, fifteen years later,
living in a house of love.
I'm going to microchip her soul
so the search will be easier next go `round.

Fifty-plus years—
haven't done too bad;
saw all my babies born,
cut the cords on two;

taught them how to enjoy good music—
Dylan and Jimmy Buffett;
good food—pizza, cheeseburgers,
chicken and dumplings like my mother made;
taught them how to ride bikes, watch horror movies,
laugh at "professional" wrestling
and tell bad jokes.
Saw them grow,
saw them go.
They all do, mine just left early.

Fifty-plus years—
where'd they go?
And why don't I feel old?

Fifty-plus years—
hell, it's only time
and it's all what you put into it.
I've crammed a lot into my small space.
I still have much to do—
finish that novel,
write that hit song,
live on a beach;
haven't given my lady
half the loving she deserves.
But that's okay,
I've got plenty of time.

No Sense

It makes no sense,
this living,
this existence,
unless you believe
one of two things:
either there is no god
or there is and
he is either
   absent minded,
      a practical joker,
         or a sadist.

If there is a god
I am not sure
I want to know him.
What kind of a benign
being would set traps
for us to condemn
ourselves to a less than
heavenly afterlife?
If he loved us,
truly, he'd make sure
we'd be perfect always.

It makes no sense to test us,
unless he takes pleasure in
such practical jokes—
like the time I told
my kid brother

I'd be right back
and he waited at
that corner forever.

Kind of like Jesus
telling us to wait for him,
he'd be back soon
to collect the just,
and we've been left
waiting here

forever.

Meaning

Someday
you'll find it
hiding from you,
afraid it will die
if found.
You'll pick it up,
brush it off,
stroke it gently
and put it
in your pocket.
And then you'll
go off whistling
down the street.

Telephone

What
do you
tell a
phone
that it
doesn't
already
know?

It's heard
it all
before.
It knows
what rings
true.

It gets
the message.
It knows
what's
connected
and what's
off the hook.

So,
what do
you tell
a phone?

Nothing.
don't trust it,
it's dropped a dime
on everyone
you know.

It's tapped
into the
party line
that sometimes
gets crossed
and leaves
you disconnected.

Descent

Dropping
down, falling
no handholds to stop
descent. How far
to the bottom?
How long ago
did I begin to fall?
Years?
So much time
as the past swirls
in the updraft,
as I plummet
to some future,
thinking,
afraid I will land,
worried I won't.

Somewhere Over the Pacific

It takes all kinds
crammed into economy class
on this massive 747
hurtling over the Pacific.
Sleep escapes us,
the evening meal and snacks
are devoured,
the feature films
have played out.
Assigned the window seat,
I have already made my two
seatmates stand
for my trips to the head.
And now,
bored,
sleepless,
I turn on the light
to read Bukowski:

> "lovely women walk by
> with big hot hips
> and warm buttocks and
> tight hot everything
> praying to be loved
> and I don't even exist."

The pretty Filipina
sitting next to me,
her petite body comfortably fitting

into the middle seat,
always a smile
when I pass my trash
to the aisle,
takes note of me turning on
the light and slips
her glasses carefully
out of a leather case
and draws a book
from the seat pocket.
I take a glance—the Bible.
She turns to Acts 3, 4.

The young Japanese man
in the aisle seat
turns on his light
and opens the latest
edition of Popular Science.
He reads about "What's New."

We are all stereotypes—
the dirty old man/poet,
the devout Catholic Filipina,
the science-minded Japanese—
on our way
to someplace else,
coming from
over there.

Roppongi

One night
while rambling
'round Roppongi,
taking the tour of Tokyo,
not knowing when
to shun the shots
of sake pressed
upon me by my friends,
down Mogumbo's
stumbling steps I slipped
and cracked my head.

Undaunted by
the bloody dent
I descended
to where some kind
soul staunched the flow
with a damp towel,
a ball cap,
and an ice cold brew.

The next morn,
co-workers, aghast
at the scabby slash
that showed through
thinning scalp,
gingerly iodined
and taped the cut,

16

wondering why
the night's itinerary
included no trip
to the emergency room.

Why? I asked.
The wet towel
ball cap
and cold, cold beer
were medicine enough.

You Too

I felt
lust
last night
while you
snored in sleep,
and awoke
to your stroke
and your smile.

You dreamed
it, too.

Fleabag Motel

Bukowski would have loved this place
a real fleabag motel; no fridge,
no ice, some cigarette-burned
ancient RCA TV bolted to a low bureau,
strips of pressed wood peeled off,
sits next to a Gideon Bible;
lamps tilt at weird angles;
chairs of ripped fake leather,
in worse shape than Salvation
Army retreads; gray-white walls marred
with black boot heel marks near the door;
dirty handprints smudge the wall near the bed;
a bullet hole marks the wall just above the TV;
the plastic covers of the electrical sockets
are cracked, split; brown water
stains on gray ceiling tiles.

Yeah, this is a Buk place, a real roach motel.
A six pack, maybe something harder,
would make it habitable.
Out back, on the other side of the parking lot,
the steady clickity clack and haunting whistle
of a freight train as it passes a crossing
makes this dump almost romantic.
Well, at least the sheets are clean.
Anyway, all I need is a place to sleep
and shower, and shit.
It's perfect for that.

Fleabag II

10:40 p.m.
Just getting settled
for bed.
Phone rings,
Hello?
"Hello, I need you to come
to the front desk."
Indian accent.
Why?
"You need to fill out
some papers."
What?
"For the police."
What?
"You need to come here,
something about your neighbor in 234."
What?
"I don't know, you need to come down here
right away."
All right.

I hang up,
confused,
put my shirt on,
grab my wallet and keys—
Whoa!
Maybe that's a bad move.
Some mugger might be waiting
just outside the door.

But I might need an ID.
I take out my money, credit cards,
slip them under the mattress.
(Strange, I'd never think of doing that in Okinawa,
but in this rundown Indiana fleabag motel,
bullet holes and boot heels marking the walls,
I worry.)

Maybe the call was a hoax,
a ploy to get me to open the door.
Wait, what if it's really the cops
and they need my contacts in this burg?
Maybe I should take my address book.
Nah, if they need them I'll just go back to the room.

I open my door,
step out,
no one around except
the trash-fed stray
cat that hangs around the stairs.
She meows loudly,
scurries away.
I descend the cracked concrete stairs,
and glance at my rented car.
No stranger there;
bright lights allow
no shadowed lairs.
I round the corner
to the front office.
The door's locked.
I spot a woman inside
waving me to a security window,

like a self-serve gas station at night.
I rap on the window
and a Paki-Indian-Bangladeshi
man walks up.
"Can I help you?"
Yeah, what do you want?
"What do YOU want?"
I dunno, someone called me,
told me to come down here
and fill out some papers.
"Sorry, no one called."
Someone did.
"Not from here, my friend."
But someone said there was a complaint
from room 234.
"I am sorry, my friend, but no one called."
No call?
"Someone did the
same thing yesterday. Sorry."

I go back to the
$25-a-night room
with mold in the shower
and crusting the
air conditioner.

I am convinced the mugger
has positioned himself
to strike when I return,
but I am greeted only
by the stray cat
in the open garbage bin.

Maybe he's already in my room,
maybe he slipped in there
while I was gone and
he's cleaned me out.
I walk around the corner
to the stairway,
stare at the door to 234—
No sign of life.
I open my door,
Silence.
No one here;
nothing missing,
just one big fucking pain in
the ass practical joke.

I've been robbed of nothing
except my sleep.

Refrigerated Moods

Magnetic Poem 1

sing
   gorgeous
      goddess
         as
             the
                 sea
                     mists.

Magnetic Poem 2

dream
   wander
      remember
         the waves
            cold yet
               blue.

Magnetic Poem 3

here
   I open
      a deep
         sleep
            vanish.

Magnetic Poem 4

child-
   like
      his
          empty
             days
                lie.

Magnetic Poem 5

ask
   friend,
      listen,
         what a
            murmur
               she was.

Magnetic Poem 6

you love
   warmly
      through
         surrender.

Magnetic Poem 7

you shall
    feel
        this gentle
            morning moment
                come
                    and turn
                        like fall
                            wind.

Magnetic Poem 8

easy neon moon
    how you burn
        like a frantic
            liquid evening
                song.

Anticipation

It comes again
not as cloudy as the dreams before,
hinting more profoundly
something new is near at hand.
I can almost touch it, outstretched
fingers slightly grazing,
hear it hiding
garbled amidst the crescendo reports
of more familiar sounds.
Who or what is this something new
sneaking around my mind's blind spot
like a cool chill on a steaming
day of city summer stranger streets?
This one hand in a dozen new
palms to shake
that feels of something more than meet?
But when or where
will the unveiling be?
Will my hopes or fears
become reality?

Mr. Paranoia

Blood circulating,
but it's doing no good,
my brain is numb and dead
from inner tension.
I stop at the spring,
but refuse to drink,
fearing some exotic infection.
Food, taste it please, I can't,
until I see you stand or fall.
It's so hard to tell
the real from
imitation.
And won't you take
this sunlight
for awhile on your skin?
I want to test it for
radiation.
Lungs breathing,
but I can't remove this mask,
after all, there might be
poison gas mixed with my
oxygen. Blood
circulating,
but it's doing no good,
my brain is dead and numb
from too much attention.

Nightmares

The cold autumn rain clouds the day,
the loneliness that follows
is not so far away, the past
never looked this real to eyes
always searching, the present
marks time to the beat of the rain.

If there is a future, it's hiding.
I find myself reaching,
riding circles on a stiff horse,
stretching for the ring.
But the ring has been stolen
and the music is confused,
there are no more childhood
memories to keep me amused.

Amusements in the park
have grown sordid and dark,
the bright lights of the funway
have faded away; where the jester
once leapt and clowns made me laugh
lies a drunk in the gutter,
empty bottle in his lap,
a smile on a booze-puttied
face no slap could sting.

The drugs which once opened
my mind to new heights are old

and taste bitter, sour sights.
What am I dreaming for
when it's only nightmares I see?

Seesaw Sensations

The seesaw sensations
of a life you sometimes
wonder is being lived,
or worth the strife,
threaten to unseat you,
accompanied by
the thud that comes
when your partner
stands, leaving you
high until the gravity
of the situation impacts.
It's then you find
the meaning of the mind.
The malaise you thought
had brought you down
was something that
you sought to face
once again, to surface
from the suffocating slights,
the fight to rise once more.

Once again victorious,
you boldly stand
and say, to no
one in particular,

"Ah, so this is living."

Gravediggers

The grave was dug almost five feet deep,
barely two feet wide,
maybe two-and-a-half feet long.
Steve and I sweated over that grave
blistering our hands,
breaking his heart.
His seed would be planted there,
a day-old son he never saw.
He never wanted a child,
but when Marylou left him
she took more than her clothes.
A son, premature, but strong
except for bad lungs.
Steve didn't know what to think,
excited at first, not every day
you have a son, even though
he'll call some other dude dad.
The birth day was a good day.
The next day, as I awoke and shuffled to the head
I passed Steve, sobbing, telephone clutched
in his shaking hand.
His baby had died unexpectedly in the night—
damn the night!
Steve, in a fog for days, almost found his way out,
but then the minister of the tiny
Episcopal church down the road
asked if Steve would dig the grave.
"After all, it was your kid," he said.
"It will save Marylou some money."

We dug that grave,
four hours in the hot sun,
ninety degrees, no shade,
with shovels, pickax,
fence post digger,
smoothing the sides,
perfect ninety-degree angles,
making ready for what the minister called
"The big send off,"
as if the baby's soul was going to wait
for his blessings before it hiked to Heaven.

Dirty and tired, we left,
met the funeral party at the graveyard gate
as we returned the minister's tools.

We spoke civilly,
Marylou looked good.
We went home, washed and took naps.
The funeral went on without us.
I had another poem.
Steve had done his penance.

Dead

Dead,
reliving the life just ended,
peeling it all back,
finally seeing;
evaluate each deed
each thought,
each act, each longing;
requited, unrequited
loves; chances taken;
easy ways out;
victories, defeats;
encouraging beginnings,
discouraging endings.
Examine,
ruminate,
evaluate,
relive each moment,
rethink each thought
(and why not? you've got
the time).
What do you find?
What have you done with your life?
And what will you do
with your death?

Organization

People give me calendars
and day books
pocket organizers
as presents.
Do they know something
about me that I refuse to face?

Nah—
I am fully aware
of my disorganized state;
I embrace it.

In my life
anarchy rules;
D doesn't necessarily
follow C
and one and one
might well be three.

My jumbled thoughts
bounce around inside
a messy mind,
a junk-filled, jumbled
room where portraits
hang askew on
muddied walls and
someone has left
the stereo and TV
playing loudly, creating

an ignored cacophonous
tinnitus ringing
in my right ear—
not my right mind,
there is no right mind,
it's left.

And so the organizers
are stuffed into
a disorganized
file drawer marked
"miscellaneous."

Underneath

Underneath a life I found,
carefully hidden there,
a spark of youth, a broken tooth
and days without a care.

David Allen

The Final Chapter

(No more novel, play, or poem similes.)

I'm leaving at the end of this chapter,
I'll vanish like the dot that ends this line.
I'm going before the novel's finished,
'cause if I stay the story's partly mine.
And I never cared too much for endings,
good or bad they all mean the same thing.
They tell you that the goddamn story's over
and I never liked the feeling "The End" brings.

I'm the character that never did develop;
a walk-on part run over by a train;
a vehicle for early romantic interest,
swept away by unexpected heavy rains.
I'm the question always left unanswered
by some glib remark made by the leading man.
I'm the patient being wheeled in on the gurney,
who dies as the leading lady holds his hand.

I never could remember the lines they gave me,
and they hated the ones ad-libbed on my own.
So, I'm giving my role to the understudy
and I'm leaving for some new stage to call home.
I'm the poem that lost its rhythm.
I'm the line that won't end in some perfect rhyme.
I'm too free-form for the tastes of the critics
I catch lurking behind me all the time.

This is the end of a long history
of poems thick with cultured similes
I'm razing all the old romantic lies.
I'm tearing down the allusions
to those chapter and verse confusions,
I'm wrecking all trace of those stale guys.

I'm going to hammer home the meanings,
no more screwing up the screenings
of the silent movies screaming in my mind.
As I buckle on my tool belt
I massage the hammer's smooth hilt
ready to nail down the message one more time.

Simply Stupid

There's a
simple
single
answer
to why
the world
is in the
mess it's in.

Stupid people.

The Glebe

Maxim, the neurotic rodent dog is
   roaming the front yard searching
      for ants to pick on.

Sammy and Angus,
   sheepdogs with friendly dispositions,
      are lying on the ground in the shade,
         bodies pressed to the earth,
            spread-eagled to
                capture the coolness.

A two lane Virginia highway
   a hundred yards from the porch
      accommodates traffic streaking
         by this calm country refuge.

Two black kids from the house out back
   walk down the driveway
      stare at this figure attached to a pen.

The wind chimes sing in the breeze as
   the stereo plays country airs broken by
      a clattering tractor in a far-off field.

A spent beer can sits on the arm
   of a wooden lawn chair, flies
      inquisitively stalking the rim.

David Allen

A barbecue grill waits
    for the sizzling dinner steaks, fat
        burgers and artery-busting hot dogs.

Stone walls surround and divide
    the cattle-tramped fields,
        waist high walls of loose flat rocks
            suggesting serener days a
                century ago when the
                    farmhouse was a
                        mansion.

A butterfly rests on the grass
    disguised as a fallen
        yellow leaf.

A door opens and someone shuffles
    out behind me on the porch,
        Claudia collecting the bent beer cans
            memories of last night's tests
            of macho-ness.

Sammy sniffs around the barbecue grill
    searching for the elusive steak,
        as from the house come the sounds
            and smells of breakfasting
            the day.

Butterflies

The butterflies
seem perfectly
content
to do nothing
more than
flitter from flower
to flower
pollinating
their lives
away.

David Allen

Impressions while driving south on I-69 from Fort Wayne to Anderson, Indiana, July 20, 2001

So, here I am
again
flat farmland
scores of semis
buckle of
the Bible Belt.
It still
sucks.

In the Country

Just sitting here,
stoned.
waiting for the frogs
to croak.

A cow moos
somewhere in the distance.
I wonder if
she thinks of time.

A candle flame flickers,
proud to be the finale
of a moth's death dance.
Neither seems to mind.

I wonder
if god
is afraid of the dark?

A Lie

Once upon a time,
I found the secret
to the truth
and,
to protect my sanity,
I smashed it
with a rock
and destroyed all trace
of the liar.

Nothing

Nothing
can never
happen.
'Cause,
if it did
something
would have
happened.

The Watcher

The watcher hovers near the crowd
hanging on the edge of the action,
observing the social animals at their game,
taking notes to future correlate
with all the observations stored before.
Quietly, he sucks it all in,
occasionally speaking a word or two.
But he's mostly gone,
wandering from room to room,
circling the circles,
searching for something,
anything, to relate to the feelings feeding,
acid eating, tearing holes in his soul.
He searches,
wanting to communicate his needs,
but he has been a searcher too long,
his quiet, out of the fear
others take for snobbishness.
He watches,
aching to be watched,
emotion burning, searing scars,
barriers between his wants
and the safety he covets.
He searches, always
on the verge of breakthrough
searching for another
watcher to share his life.

True Lies

Many are the times
   that I have
      lied to tell
         the truth.

Many are the times
   that they have
      stretched a truth
         to lie.

Timing

Went to the dentist the other day
and as he prepared
me for a root canal
I checked out his new goatee.

"Growing that so your patients
won't recognize you
when you go out in public?"
I asked. Not even a smile.

A pain-filled hour later
it dawned on me
that I never did have
a good sense
of comedic timing.

My Howl

*(By Dylan, the Poetry Dog, with an
English Translation by David Allen)*

I saw the best pups of my litter
petted, pawed at, pulled
from Mom's teat too soon.
crammed in cages, placed on view,
prices posted on paper-lined lairs,
dens barely large enough to
turn around. Sold to strangers,
shampooed, collared, carted away
from cage-mates in cars, transported
to new dens ruled by bipeds.
Lonely without litter mates,
we tried to play puppy games.
But our friendly greeting bites
were met with shrill shouts,
"No bite! No bite!"
No bite?
What do they want us to do?
Lie still while the world awaits,
to taste, to smell, to roll in?
Hide our excitement? Be rude?
Passively accept the patting hand,
the petting massage, with
no teeth? To bite the hand
that feeds you is not a crime,
but a compliment. We do not tear at their flesh,

but mouth them, teeth and tongue
become a part of them, forming a we.
Ahh, but bipeds think too slow,
can't broadcast their thoughts,
or receive, no matter how hard we try to send.
They cannot talk to wind, to leaves, to grass,
to the pack with thoughts.
They bark, but never bite.
What sin did they commit to
have to keep their thoughts to themselves?
Bipeds! Hapless bipeds!
You treat my brothers sorely,
You speak with shouts and coos,
Commands and tempt us with treats,
but we know of Pavlov and his bells.
We trained him. Who was it got to eat?
Bipeds! You can chain us, but never own us.
You can cage our bodies, but our minds run free.
Bipeds! We will shake your hand,
come when called,
chase your balls,
catch your Frisbees,
but remember always, it's our choice
when to obey and when to run.
The wild dog you invited to share
your campfire is within us still.
Bipeds! Hear our growls. Know
you may drive some of us crazy,
you may take the mad ones,
outcast, abandoned ones away,
cage us together one last time
in death-row kennels;

put us to that never waking sleep,
to sleep, perchance to dream, of freedom
that you can never know.
Bipeds! You may force us to
act the fool; dress us as clowns,
make us look ridiculous,
cut our hair in weird designs,
dye our ears, bob our tails, but
you cannot conquer our spirit.
For—I saw the best pups of my litter,
spirit-filled, running free, despite leash and cage.
For we are what you bipeds can never be—
We are dogs!

Typewriter Rhythm

He sits at the typewriter
tap, tap, tap dancing,
his fingers playing rhythm,
his mind swirling on the dance floor.
His muse,
fruit hat balanced on her head,
is warm to his touch at her waist
as they dip, slide, turn and glide
the night away.
Tap, tap, tap,
the thoughts form into letters, words
staccatoing the beat;
faster, faster, building
intense, the dancers fling about the floor,
around and down, around, around
and up.
Tap, tap, tap,
fingers madly lightly touching
electric dancing keys,
until, at last, the climax comes
and the musicians play
"Goodnight Ladies,"
as silence sweeps the dance floor clean
(except for the motor's hum).

Requiem for My Father

Jeannie called and said
"David, Dad's dead.
He fell and bumped his head."
And inside I bled
   for a man long dead
        in memories
              of a family
                    that used to be.

Jeanie was calm.
She said our Mom
was all right,
though "she just sat and stared."
And I cried then,
   but I don't know why when
        you had died ten,
                twenty years ago.

You had fled
to your dark bed-tomb
and you left that crypt,
that stenched of rotting dreams
and surrender,
only for soft drinks
and to pee.

So, I called Ricky, the youngest,
and he said no tears tracked his cheeks.
"I'd been telling everyone
my Dad died years ago," he said.

Ricky said:
"I once asked Dad what he was going to do today.
   He said: Nothin'.
I said what about tomorrow?
   And he said: Nothin'.
And I asked him how could he give up
after surviving World War II and alcohol?
   And he said: Leave me alone.
And I told him he had to leave his room or die
   And he said: Ricky, I only leave the room to pee.
And I repeated, if you don't leave the room you'll die.
   And he said: Nobody can tell me what to do."

Nobody could.

Mom wrote last week,
said you were doing less
and less for yourself;
that Kathy had come by to shave you;
that you and Mom were to celebrate
your 50th wedding anniversary.
She said she didn't know how you two
had stayed together so long.

You didn't.

'Til death did you part.
But which death?
This final, no-breath death of today?
Or the thousand times you died since the war?
We, your children, are the products
of the half-man, half-soldier, Mom welcomed home.

The best part was left in the rubble
of a bomb-shattered wine cellar near Bastogne.
You were the sole survivor of your squad,
a heavy burden to bring back home,
a burden laid on your children.

The tag you wore around your neck
when you awoke in some hospital,
safe behind the lines said:
   "This man is not responsible
      for his actions."

You never were.

You never recovered.
Booze, your best buddy,
carried you through your days—
   from job to job,
      child to child,
         town to town.

At least we older children have memories
of a man, crippled perhaps, yet still struggling
still searching to retain some semblance of living;
pictures of a smiling man in a fireman's dress blues
posturing before a neat Levittown bungalow.
Flash forward:
   a man in shabbier clothes,
      tilted cowboy hat, sad smile,
         playing a mandolin in a boozy haze—
            yet picking those strings,
               making her sing.

But never loud nor long enough to heal the wounds.

In poverty, Mom raised us
as you struggled with your demons;
your days haunted by ghosts of what were
and could have been.
I left home first,
tasted the salt sea air of freedom
and returned to find another man
wearing my father's clothes.

You were booze free, but hooked on pills
that still could not ease your pain.

Twenty more years passed
and you became another kind of Dad
for the younger ones.
No more booze,
no more belts across bare buttocks.
You went to AA and, for awhile, held court
at the dinner table,
telling bad jokes and drinking soda.

But your nerves were shot,
you couldn't work,
only the pill-induced sleep stopped the demons.
You retreated from the world,
no more morning walks for the paper,
no more evening talks at the table.
The bed tomb beckoned.

The tube flickered in the dark,
images of the world you turned your back on.

These last years
we visited Mom and brought reluctant children
into your cave to say
Hi and Bye to their Pop
   (I never called you that).
They cringed to see the unwashed man
   with inch-long toenails,
      shaggy hair,
         swollen Buddha belly,
           glazed eyes.

My kids don't remember much, Dad.
But I'll try to recreate the memories.
I'll tell them about the war hero;
   the tank killer;
      the high school football star;
         the cartoonist;
           the musician;
              the man;
the slender Yankee with the toothy grin
   and easygoin' manner that
      swept our Southern Mom off her feet
      and into the Allens.

I'll remember for them
   the demon-less Dad
      I tell myself
      was hiding there
         all along.

Mandolin Therapy

My father plays the mandolin
when life begins to close him in;
playing old folk tunes and country airs,
music helps to soothe his cares
and ease his life.

And he plays,
    when the need for drink
    clouds his brain
    and he can't think.

He plays,
    when the bills are high
    and cash is low
    when my mother cries.

He plays,
    into the night
    but it never seems
    to come out right.

He plays the mandolin
when life begins to close him in.

He plays.

I Never Wrote a Poem About My Mother

I never wrote a poem
about my mother,
even though dozens about dad
flowed from pens filled
with ink blood red.
After all, he planted the seeds
of fear and hopelessness, deep
strong roots grown in furrows
slashed into pliant flesh
by belts stinging,
quick backhands,
cutting words, while
mom protested in silence,
condoning the conditioning years
later saying—
"But afterwards he always cried."

I never wrote a poem for my mother,
though I love her and think fondly
of the bond we formed in later years.
What was there to write?
I tried to protect her once.
I was nine and my Dad, drunk again,
had raised his hand one too many times
and, as he stumbled from the house,
my mom damning him to the fiery pit,
I chased him down the steps,
swatting his back with the brush end of a broom;
trying to sweep him from our lives,
I suppose, though he's here still

long after buried in a veteran's grave.
I never wrote a poem
about my mother.
She kept us together somehow
all those years, for what
I never understood.
I relished the times
I was farmed out to
uncles, aunts and my
Nan's strong, protecting arms.

I never wrote a poem about my mother
who never told me what to be;
just follow the rules,
as muddled as they are.
"Stay out of trouble, David
or you'll anger you father."
He was so quick to anger,
haunted by war ghosts
and failures too numerous to name;
a dozen jobs, a dozen homes,
a dozen shattered promises.
I stood with her often on the welfare lines,
bringing home the state dole of
oily peanut butter in gallon cans,
powdered milk, cornmeal
and the white beans that gagged me
every time.

I never wrote a poem for my mother,
though she saved me once by moving us
to another county when
the streets beckoned and threatened

to steal the soul of her oldest son.
She never said why we moved
and I always assumed it was to hide
from the collection agents who came
round to our door as often
as the milkman and the mail.

I never wrote a poem to my mother,
who, behind the scenes later
cut the strings, let me find my own way,
any way that was better than
the stifling daily struggle.
She suffered alone with seven
children and failing health.

I never wrote a poem about my mother
who, stoically now in her Golden Years,
a widow, children grown, has finally
allowed herself to live her own life, with no regrets,
no sighs of could-have-beens, but says,
"That's just the way things were
and I did the best I could."

I never wrote a poem for my mother
who never taught me to hug,
or love, but managed still
to make sure we always had food
and clothes and a bed, where in dreams
I escaped the dread of the Dad-filled days
until I was strong enough to run.

I never wrote a poem for my mother
and still I wonder why?

We Don't Know Death

"My daddy died," she said,
And I embraced her.
"I know," I said.
But I didn't really.
How can any of the living
know death?
We know only the absence
of a loved one;
perhaps a name in an obituary.
When the curtain falls
we all just clap, in a way,
as if to say,
"That was a good life,
Good for you."
Then we're left waiting
for the next act.

Running

It's always been different for me,
learning to be a loner,
yearning to be needed.

The eldest of seven
in a family of madness,
making my fortress from books;
fleeing into histories,
adopting biographies,
puzzling over philosophies,
making the myths mine,
fantasizing the fictions,
until I poked my mind into poetry
and became found.

But poetry doesn't pay the rent,
choices had to be made
to feed the body
as the rhymes,
from haikus to sonnets
soothed my soul.

I chose a journalist's guise,
selling truth—four bits a copy.
Writing to pay the rent,
writing to feed the soul,
not a bad life.

But it was rough
in the beginning.
The book walls crumbled
and, crippled, I learned to crawl
away; flee on foot, bike,
car, train, ship and plane,
ever further away.
But evil always found me in the west.
(Evil backwards, after all,
is live, and just trying to
get by was always complicated.)
Bills and lost loves accumulated
putting me in debt,
the constant calls for capitulating
to society's expectations
pushed me further and further west,
the soul, shrunken from the sheer
weight of life, screamed.

Journalistic burnout—
one too many murders,
crack kids settling scores
with nine millimeter un-peacemakers,
automatic fire crackling
in central city cocaine streets.
Mid-life crisis circus—
mad wife descending into
the pit of her personal hell,
aided by therapists
bent on proving Satan does exist.
Divorce, disclosures

that life's discourse
was off course again.

Sometimes the only answer is to run
straight into a new encounter.
A latter-life love,
it took ten years for that
ship's shakedown cruise
to bring us to this paradise port,
the end of one voyage,
the skipping of states, regions,
continents, oceans,
and the beginning of a new
more leisurely course.

We dropped our anchor in Asia
so, far it seems,
that if we went any further
we'd be running back.

With Love on His Lips

He died with love on his lips,
whispering, " I love you,"
to his bride of 64 years,
who sat by his side as he slipped
away to what follows.
Simple, stubborn, a farmer
and man of few words but many
good deeds; so lovingly
remembered that old friends
some strangers for decades,
crowded the funeral chapel,
forcing it to remain open
hours beyond schedule.
He had plowed deep
furrows of friendship,
now reaped upon his passing.
His family gathers today from
the far corners of the country
to the Hoosier homestead he built
with his two god-fearing hands,
to mark his crossing over,
but not his absence from their lives.
A half world away, we who
could not be there also celebrate
his life with his favorite meal and pastime—
being with family and friends
at the dinner table at the end of a long day—life.

The Names

George Allen White Jr.,
  Edward Lewis White,
    James White...

Names,
American Marines who died on Okinawa.
These names are read in June,
in April the names were soldiers,
May was for sailors.

Names
every day.

On April 1,
the reading of the names began
to commemorate
April fool's Day,
Easter Sunday,
Love Day,
the day the Americans invaded Okinawa,
struck back on Japan's home soil
in 1945.

Every day
for an hour at lunch
and in the evening
they came to read the names
at a church high on a hill
overlooking the invasion beaches.

A church with American and Japanese
    parishioners,
with a Japanese-Canadian priest,
who spent his war in a cold Saskatchewan
internment camp.
Every day
they come to
All Souls Episcopal Church
to read the names of the souls
lost.

James Preston White,
    James Thomas White,
        Jerry Wilson White...

They are coming to the end.
Eighty-three days,
each day of the battle.
Returning veterans,
some with wives and grown children,
sit in the back of the chapel.
Silent.
Respectful.

Thousands of names.
    12,281 Americans,
        110,000 Japanese soldiers and
            Okinawan conscripts,

More than 150,000 Okinawa civilians.

Logan Willard White Jr.,
Thomas George White,
Charles Edward Whiteman...

Each name another soldier,
sailor, aviator, civilian
killed in the carnage that was
the Battle of Okinawa.
Listen .

James Richard Whiteman,
Mark Edward Whiteman,
Forrest Whitt,
Joseph Henry Whitaker...

Whisper them softly,
fall into the rhythm.
it's a Jewish Kaddish,
a Buddhist chant,
a Christian prayer.
Meditate.

Joseph Henry Whittaker,
Marvin Jones Wiggins,
William Robert Wiggins...

Name after name.
Each man some mother's son,
some father's pride.
This one the class clown;
that one the brain.

Some were orphans,
no family except their platoon
or shipmates.
That guy was a Gary steelworker,
and wasn't little Jimmy Whit
the mechanic down at the corner garage?

And what of the names read
on other days?

David Bond,
   Earl Graham,
      Ernie Pyle...

Wait, that one's familiar.
Pyle, a newspaperman,
he wrote about these people,
always making sure he got the names right.
Thousands of names for the readers back home,
'til a Japanese sniper reaped his name
for the book of the fallen.
All-American
names.

Howard S. Schwartz,
   Louis Odachowski,
      Kazuyoshi Inouye...

Some of the veterans are uneasy
on the wooden church pews,
it's hard to sit through;

the reader's voice is hoarse,
so many names.

Robert Wiggins,
   Gray Huntley Whitman,
      Hugh Whittington...

So many names.
Names inscribed on a striking monument
on Mabuni Hill, where the Japanese Army
made its last stand.
The Cornerstones of Peace,
the names of the dead from all the countries,
carved into 1,200 black granite walls,
stretching to the sea
like the wings of doves.

Donald James Wilton,
   Kenneth William Wilkins,
      Jack Williard...

The American list is over for the day.
The veterans leave,
handkerchiefs pat at moist eyes.
Few remain in the chapel
as a new reader sits at the table.
She begins to read.

Sato Yoshiro,
   Yasuoka Tomohiko,
      Murakami Minoru...

More names.
These are Japanese,
a college conscript from Tokyo,
a farmer from Hokkaido,
soldiers in the Emperor's Army on Okinawa
when the Americans came with their
Typhoon of Steel.

Pak Man-do,
   Chou Che-jiu,
      Song Yong...

Korean names,
forced laborers,
comfort women.

Masahiro Kohagura,
   Masao Ota,
      Kiyo Yamashiro...

Okinawa names,
Page after page.
It sometimes takes 10 minutes
to read the day's American names,
25 minutes for the Japanese,
much longer for the Okinawans.
That name belonged to a fisherman from Kin.
And wasn't that the name of the mother from
Itoman who huddled in fear
at the rear of a deep cave with her two children,
shivering with fright as death came calling,
collecting his names?

Grandfathers,
babies,
teenage girls pressed into service to tend
the wounded.
Whole families of names,
each a sad reminder of War's toll;
each name a testament.
To what?

Life.
This person once lived.
"I existed,
I had a name,
I was somebody."

Read our names,
remember us.

Behind the Headlines

"Okinawa in Turmoil
In Airman Rape Case"

That's the headline.
The reality?
Twenty protesters gather
at the air base's front gate
shout slogans,
shake fists,
then hop the bus and stop
for burgers at McDonald's.
Politicians in Naha
do the dance of the outraged
and make plans for more
Gomen money from Tokyo.
Maybe they'll use it
to pave another road to nowhere.
My neighbor, Eizo,
descended from kings,
walks into Paul's pad
outraged.
Outraged the *gaijins*
who rent his cabins
don't appreciate his favorite beer.
"Budweiser number one!
Budweiser *ichiban!*"
he shouts.
Paul, an Irishman from London, laughs

"Bud number ten!" he shouts
and offers the King of Iha,
standing there barefoot in a white tee-shirt and
blue work pants, his glass of Guinness.
"Slante,'" Paul toasts. "Drink this."
"No, no," Eizo laughs. "No good."
They compromise with glasses
of Okinawa awamori over ice.
Another international dispute settled.

Okinawa Morning

7 a.m., the sun rises lazily over Ishikawa,
blazing yellow bands of sunlight
spread apart the curtain of clouds
that enclosed the city in darkness;
suffused sunbeams cast rays
upon the warm waters of the bay,
where an oil tanker glides slowly
over the mirror-smooth surface,
winding its way to a finger of a pier
jutting out from the rocky shore.
Up here, on a hill far above the awakening
city, a hawk slips by on an updraft
and mourning doves coo,
silencing the tree frogs and geckos
who cloaked the night with their croaking.
When the cooing halts, wind
caresses jungle foliage. Directly below,
no one invades the calm of the dew-covered
golf course, its luscious greens pale
compared to the hundred shades of green
of jungle, sugar cane and tea fields
blanketing the land leading to the bay.
Yellow hibiscus flowers open
and bid "*Ohaiyo gozaimasu, genki desu ka?*"

Ah, it's morning at the Cabin Serendip
and all is "*genki desu.*"

March Mischief

The sun has returned,
the light's too bright
after months of clouds.
We have lived through
several Februarys,
sun deprivation,
as the clouds and rain
dampened our spirits,
drugged us into
a somnambulistic shuffle,
merely marking the days,
the heatless hours,
cold nights in the subtropics.
Shivering, she screamed,
"Next year we winter in Guam!"
And headed undercover.
But now, all's forgiven
as the sun warms us,
lulls us into shorts, bare feet,
ice cold beers in the afternoon,
lounging on the lawn
soaking in the rays,
building up the base
for nose blisters,
flaking foreheads.
All the while, Sol smiles
mischievously, knowing
the rainy season is just weeks away.

The Last Sunset of the 20ᵗʰ Century

I watched the sun set on the last day
of the century behind an anvil-shaped cloud
over the East China Sea
and wondered if that meant something.
That dark cloud, dampening the brilliant yellows
and oranges that usually trumpet the sunset's finale;
a huge black thing looming over
this entry into the new millennium—
closing the door on the last century,
scarred by so much war and devastation.
A black anvil—darkness impenetrable
by even the power of the sun?
Or an anvil on which to beat
swords into plowshares at last,
the century of wars surrendering
to a time of peace. Or, it means
no more than the random numbering
of the years: 5760 by the Hebrew calendar;
close to the Year of the Dragon, the 17ᵗʰ year
of the 78ᵗʰ cycle of the Chinese calendar;
1378 if Allah is your god. What to make
of the Millennium hype? The Y2K scare?
As I write this, the fireworks are over
in Christchurch and Sydney
and the lights are still on.
Later on, my love and I
will wander outside to watch
the fireworks from Katsuren

as Okinawa ushers the New Year in—
the 12th year of the Heisei Era, I think.
Then we'll sip some champagne.
Abed, we'll celebrate our own benchmark—
our 12th year togetherness.

Now, that's something real to cheer.

Club Red

I am still trying
to figure out what
Sesame Street is
all about, playing
on the TV screens
over the bar.
Last time I wandered
in here there were
young college co-eds
showing their titties
at some X-rated Spring Break.
Now I watch
Conjunction Junction
and figure, hell,
both videos make some
kind of perverted sense
at Open Mike poetry night
at the Club Red.

Daily News

No news today
I'm on vacation;
slept late,
no daily work routine,
no papers to read,
no e-mail to answer,
no radio, TV or
Internet news reports
to slog through.
I'm free.

Until the cell phone rings.
An editor from a thousand
miles away says something
big happened today,
can I drop the nothing
I am doing and log-on?
Make some phone calls?
Get some reaction,
find some local color,
something new to feed
the copy beast?
Can I crank out something
for the next news cycle?

Sure, I say, what the hell,
maybe nothing will happen
tomorrow.

What I Did on My Summer Vacation in October

(Or Someone Painted the Pig's Balls Blue)

Prelude:

> The paycheck stub
> says use or lose
> so, I choose
> vacation—
> V-A-C-A-T-I-O-N
> This is how it went.

Day One:
> I read poems
> and the earth moves.
> Miles below us
> the earth rocks—
> no connection.
> "The crowd was
> pretty silent," I say,
> returning to my seat.
> "We were all wondering
> whether to run," Ruth
> Ellen answers.
> Again, no connection.

Day Two:
> Sunday
> rain followed by rain
> with a little more rain,

a drowsy, kind of
sleep in day to make
the transition to vacation.
Pizza Man,
up to his ankles in water,
braving the flood,
delivering the meatrageous.
Diets be damned,
we're on vacation!

Day Three:
Rain at dawn;
what a surprise!
It rains cats and dogs,
fish and frogs,
it pours in buckets,
falls straight in sheets,
it rains blankets—
hell, it rains the whole damn mattress.
We shop for last
minute things and buy
what impulse brings.

Day Four:
Off for the fair shores of Okuma,
north island mountains,
sandy seashore. We're off
to bathe ourselves in sunshine.
But first, we must survive the rain.
It rains so hard
we can't tell sea from sky
and the road is a river

of water looking
for an open drain.
Kadena Circle is a fog of spray,
cars fishtail, wipers
futilely beat at the rain,
slapping time to
a Buffett refrain.
At the Kina slaughterhouse
and restaurant someone
painted the pig's balls blue.
An omen, 'cause just outside
of Nago the blue sky
breaks through.
Mountains steamy,
wisps of clouds play
in and out the window
through the folds.
Salvador Dali slopes,
cement slabs slide
down the mountainside—
no falling rocks here.

The road narrows,
double lanes hug the coast.
Shioya Bridge, it pleases me
to drive through your bright red arches
before your featureless brother
takes your place.

And then—Okuma!
"No bottled beverages
allowed in this facility."

Quick, hide
the long-necked Becks.

Ruth Ellen, trusted
navigator, willing scribe,
says the poem's taking
epic proportions:

By the shores of great Okuma
I bit deep into my burger,
burger smothered rich with mushrooms
covered with a coat of cheese.
I bit deep into my burger
and let out a moan of pleasure,
startling my lunch companion
who said, "Well, I see you're pleased.
You never moan so loud when
 we're together doing the dance
 of mare and stallion;
(oh, the pickle and the onion)
no, you never moan so loud
on the nights we roll in bed."
I could only nod my head,
for I was no Indian brave
and it was the Cheeseburger
in Paradise that I had craved
since before the trip began.

Day Five:
 Inaccuweather calls for
 scattered showers
 interrupted by torrents.

During a sun break, we
try snorkeling, but
Mother Ocean's strong current
threatens to carry us away.
"Not yet, not today!"
we shout, as we leave Robinson Crusoe
footprints in the sand.
"There's adventure ahead.
We're on vacation, damn it!"

The way to beat the clouds
is to drive into them.
Cross Highway 58,
past the turnoff to Higa Falls,
and up, up, up
the snaking mountain road
that twists and turns
like a woman's body,
caressing the curves,
finessing them with convex
mirrors, we drive through
the clouds forming
in the valleys below.

Mile, after mile
and not another soul.
At spots the jungle threatens
to reclaim the road,
eliminate all trace of the
concrete ribbon rising
up, up, up,
and around and down

and up again.
A little-traveled trail,
a patchy asphalt one-lane
almost-path branches
off, beckons.
Dare we take it?
Dare we not?

Our Honda Shuttle
was not made for such
adventure, but handles
well the trail, so unused
that at parts vast spider
webs—spider condos—
block our passage.
Rain droplets, like diamonds,
hang from the silk.
Ruth Ellen gently
brushes them aside
with a big stick.
Hard work,
the intricate webs
are strongly anchored
and she is sprung back
a few attempts
before she clears a path.
"I didn't want to ruin
such art," she says
as we roll onward,
ever upward, under
the canopy of trees.

Suddenly, bright yellow posts
mark the edge of the trail.
"USMC," they are stamped.
We wonder what that means?
But no one said "Keep Out."
So we continue our climb.
Beside us, steep drops
down the rocky, jungle slopes.
We stop and stand at the edge
and all we see is a
carpet of green, mile after
mile of mountain,
   inviting,
         embracing,
              nurturing.

We stand, and with
upraised arms we shout,
"Top O' the world, Ma!
   Top O' the World!"

The trail ends abruptly,
an anticlimax at
a barbed-wired U.S.
Army enclosure,
a microwave tower,
concrete and steel
monstrosity, way out
of place here in Heaven.

Reluctantly, we turn and trek
back down the trail

of the banana spiders.
On the main road,
on a rare straight stretch,
a sign in kanji and English shouts:
"Speed Down!"
Of course!
Speed down!
There is no incessant voice
from Tokyo, some editor
demanding 10 more inches
of copy in 15 minutes.
There's no newshole
for the newswhores to fill.
Speed Down! and smell the—
well, hibiscus and pineapple
will have to substitute for
fabled roses.
Speed Down!
and smell the ocean.
"Speed Down!" it shouts,
"You're on vacation."

Day Six:

A bad body day means spending the time
inside, reading to my soul-mate as she
fights the phantom pain the disease insists
is the price for a few pain-less, or rather
less pain-filled days.
    (Pain and fatigue play
    their game upon the field
    that is her body;
    sometimes, like soccer,

scoreless, some sweet succor,
sometimes running up the score.
They are in double digits today.)

Yet, she still serves me a grimace
with a smile chaser as I
read her to sleep—
e. e. cummings'
"I six non-lectures,"
A book borrowed from
a new young poet friend
just discovering his muse
(how I envy the paths he has yet to tread,
the poems and books yet to be read).

And in the reading,
while she dozes and wakes,
drifts in and out of painfulness
I discover cummings'
non-lecture on what
a poet is:

 "If you wish to follow
 even at a distance,
 the poet's calling…
 you've got to come out
 of the measurable doing universe
 into the un-measurable house of being.
 If poetry is your goal
 you've got to forget
 all about punishments and
 all about rewards and

all about self-styled obligations
and duties and responsibilities
etcetera ad infinitum
and remember one thing only—
that it's you, nobody else, who
determines your destiny and decides
your fate.
Nobody else can live for you,
nor can you live for anyone else."

And so, I read to my wife,
my muse, my partner in
life's discourse and spend
the most pleasurable day
of my vacation.

At night, dinner with a sunsct for dessert.
The thing I like about sunsets best
is, just as the leading lady leaves the stage,
the whole sky explodes in colorfulness,
an ovation for another day well done.
My love loves best
this dimming of the day,
when all cares and pain
like butter melt away
and, like an old friend,
the night comes to cloak our nakedness
with a fine silk robe.

Day Seven:
On the Seventh Day I wish
I could say we rested,

but instead we drove
as the sun shone strong
back home to where our worries
and cares waited, pouting children
mad we didn't take them along.

Another Night

Woke up on the couch
again.
Head aches,
stomach's queasy,
bladder's bulging.
Sit up,
sends my head spinning.
And, man, what happened to my thumb?
Feels sprained must've jammed it.
How?
And what's this?
Front of my shirt like cardboard,
something wet dried.
Takes me three tries to stand,
feel dizzy,
stumble to the head.
Ahhhh, that feels good,
you know, you just kind of rent beer.
Wash my hands, look in the mirror—
Jeezus!
Right side of my temple's all bruised,
throbbing,
nerves send a ditto from my right knee.
It's all scraped and scabbed.
Must've fallen somewhere,
somehow,
sometime.
Don't remember.
Re awakens, comes downstairs,

tells me I crawled into the house
at 4:30 in the morning.
Kept shouting
"Leave me alone,
I don't want you to see me
like this. Go 'way."
She says something about a guzzling tequila
contest with the last holdouts,
trying to eat the worm.

Hours later,
cleaning the mess on the porch
I find the worm.
Looks like I won.

Housekeeping Haiku

Many more dead ants
    cover my table, they rain
        down, a summer storm.

David Allen

Horticulture Haiku

Pretty rock gardens
   so popular in Japan
      no damn grass to mow.

Cold War

The Cold War's over
we can all apply
for our certificates of accomplishment
at: http://coldwar.army.mil
It's official.

It seems so easy
these days to be a hero.
You can bet I did my part
to win the Cold War,
nervously patrolling
the narrow harbor streets of
St. Thomas and Old San Juan,
a 5-foot-2-inch sailor
armed with a blue SP armband
and a billy club that
I used to smash flies
and tap a tabletop rhythm
to the loud-ass rock band
that played at the Lucky Seven,
the Gator Sailors' bar
just up the hill from the waterfront.

Yeah, the Cold War's over.
I was surprised to learn
I had earned my very own certificate.
It states: "In recognition
of your service
during the Cold War,

2 September 1945, to
26 December 1991,
in promoting peace and
stability for this nation,
the people of this nation
are forever grateful."

Well, no one ever said
bureaucrats can write poetry.

Grateful.
Grateful to me
for saving Pilar from communism
teaching her good old American
capitalism—
five for her
two for the room.

Grateful for me that day back in '68,
when some dumb-ass gunners mate
in Panama gave me that blue armband
and a club and a .45 and
told me and a bunch of other
land-sick sailors just come back
from a 24-hour pass to Panama City,
fresh from a 24-hour drunk,
to stand by, that
we might be needed for riot duty
if those "communist fuckers" from Colon
bring their anti-American demonstration
to the base.
They never came,

which was good,
'cause all I ever had done with a .45 before
was to play quick draw with
the guy on the quarterdeck of the ship
across the pier from mine.

A couple of years later
I did my part to win the Cold War
by marching with thousands of angry Vietnam vets,
guys with better credentials than I
for being opposed to a war that all but God and
     LBJ
had forsaken and
Tricky Dick expanded.
Certificate doesn't say
anything about that,
but I believe those heady days
of marching in the streets
should count.
We drove the Pentagon so crazy
that you can bet we won't
be bogged down in a war like that again.

(Not until the memories fade, anyhow.)

I'm going to hang my certificate
on a wall, framed with a picture
of me and the boys
from the Sufferin' Suffolk (LST1173),
toasting ourselves
to another successful
night of liberty.

I'd add my sole medal,
or at least the yellow and red ribbon
that went with it—
you know, the medal for
"National Defense,"
the one they gave everyone for
surviving boot camp.
But that medal and ribbon joined
a pile of other medals
chucked over the barricades
protecting the Capitol steps
from the Vietnam Vets.
They joined the purple hearts
and the bronze and silver stars
and other medals for gallantry
and heroism in an act above and
beyond any duty they did in the Nam.
That was a day! A heroic day!
The cherry blossoms bloomed,
even the police smiled
that day in the Spring of 1971,
when the attention of the nation
was focused on Vietnam
and the Cold War
was left to, well,
grow colder.

Yeah,
Think I'll frame that certificate
hang it
right next to my

Honorable Discharge.
Show I did my part,
beat those Russians,
helped Uncle Sam bankrupt the bastards
by building the
mightiest military
the world's ever seen.

So, next time you see me,
give me that old Peace sign,
or the right-on clenched fist
thrust into the air.
I won the Cold War
and I've got the certificate to prove it.

Sailor's Lament

(or, five for me, two for the room)

Sleazy, cheap
and on the downslide of life.
I wish there was a way to say
I'd like to be your friend.
But this is Old San Juan
and I am just a sailor
with five and two.

Sometimes to Love

Sometimes to love
you have to leave,
you have to let alone.
To turn around
and walk away is
the hardest thing I've known.

Kosovo Is in Flames

("Eat your peas, dear.")

Every night we see them
ruining our supper,
sad eyes pleading,
praying for help,
fleeing with what little
clothing and dignity they have
to a foreign border land
because some Serb
didn't like the way they spelled
their name or the god they prayed to.
There's really not much more
of a difference between them.

Don't they bother you?
Don't you wish they were near
so you could take them in,
feed them, clothe them
hug them, love them
give them shelter from the genocidal storm
of Serb guns and Bics and NATO bombs?

Sometimes, when the bombs are falling
it's hard to tell who is your friend
until the jet jockeys jerk
their winged Horsemen of the Apocalypse home
and your Serbian neighbor

in a black mask and militia uniform
says. "Look, they missed your home,
let me burn it for you.
Look, you still have valuables,
let me take them from you.
Look, your son and husband still live,
let me kill them for you.
Look, you still have your dignity,
let me rape you.
Let me relieve you of your burden,
lighten your load
for that long walk through the mountains
to the refugee camps."

They clear Kosovo of Albanians
as efficiently as McDonald's
makes Big Macs.
Look—one million Kosovars
Serbed today.

Today I cry for the Kosovars,
yesterday it was the Bosnians;
last year the Rwandans earned my tears.
Do I have more for Timor?
The Sudanese? The Congolese?
Death is reaping a bounteous harvest
as we watch it all on TV,
so insensitive, so removed.
It doesn't ruin our appetites any more
unless an American plane is shot down
or one of our soldiers are captured,

or has his naked, lifeless body dragged
through a cheering crowd down
some strange Somalian street.

And if it does upset us,
we can always turn it off,
change the channel.
There's a comedy on Showtime,
that's the way to watch a war.

Kosovo is In Flames: Part II

Revenge is sweet.
No, that's not right,
it's sour,
a stench fills the air.
Serb homes burn in the moonlight;
Serb blood soaks the soil.
The fighting continues,
the tit-for-tat tearing the country apart.
Centuries of pain permeate this land,
there is no peace possible,
nothing can grow, except hate.
It bubbles up, it boils, embroiled passions
plague this peace-poor place.
"We won (with the help of NATO)!"
the Kosovo Albanians triumphantly cry,
"Now it's your turn to die;
now it's your turn to turn over the loose soil
of unmarked graves;
now it's your turn to flee in tractor drawn trailers
piled high with the few goods you have time to pack.
Now it's our turn to joy ride in the Mercedes
taken from our enemy;
now it's our turn to make children fatherless;
wives husbandless; families homeless."
Madness manifests itself in the minds of those
huddled in the hills only a few months before,
running from the same kind of ethnic cleansing
they now scrub across the countryside.
They cheered the Americans as their tanks

109

rumbled through their towns,
never understanding the moral principles
of those soldiers from the melting pot nation,
where ethnic purity is a cry
taken up by a handful, a miniscule minority
of half-baked fascists in brown shirts.
The soldiers defending them come from a rainbow
of ethnic and cultural backgrounds, armed with an
understanding that everyone has a right to live
in peace, pursue happiness, enjoy domestic
tranquility.
We should have balked at the Balkans,
there is no cure for the disease infecting this land.
Today my tears are now for the Serbs.
Tomorrow?

9/11/01

Terrorists took
security away
from Americans today.

Now we're as scared
as a bus rider
in Jerusalem,
a shopkeeper in Derry,
a banker in Basque,
a Hindu in Kashmir,
a Muslim in Serbia.

Now, we're all scared—
welcome to the terror-ble times.

Smile

Fingers tracing
lazy lines along
the curves of you.

Smile for me now
we've become the friends
you feared the sex would shun.
Smile for me now,
we've breached the outer walls
and have become
more than we dreamed.
Smile for me now
and let tomorrow
take care of itself;
dark yesterday has
yielded to today.

Tongues dancing
inside mouths refreshed
by love's sweet dew.

Last Night

Last night I slept in sheets made damp
by love in the hot afternoon.
The pillow where you lay your head,
I held close to my side.
A dreaming smile upon my lips,
I touched your pale, soft skin.
Your body arched as fingers found
the spring of love within.
Softly stroking, gentle touch,
you held me, pressing close.
Our juices mixed as body's joined
we moaned and slowly danced.
You whispered my name as I sighed yours,
your kiss tickled my ear.
I opened my eyes to drink in yours,
but, you were nowhere near.
A daytime love is all we have.
I moved the pillow away
and waited for the sun
to chase this loneliness.

Words

Words, where are you now?
I need you evermore,
as weaponless I'll never stand
my ground against
the hordes of doubt.
Words, where are you now?
Cupid's arrow never struck as deep
as with the poems and prose
I used to send walls tumbling to the ground.
Words, where are you now?
The masons have moved in,
they are making repairs,
expanding, fortifying the fortress,
raising the walls too high,
I cannot see the lofty turrets for the clouds.
Too high, too high,
and windowless.
Words, where are
you now?
Armorless, I stand undefended,
no more circles of logic,
no more battering rams of
argument to ram through the gates,
no more words—
where are you now?
You once marched freely
from the nib of my pen,
prepared to tear down the walls
again and again,

no quarter,
ever pressing onward—
but words where
are you now
that I need you?
To fight the good fight.
Tonight.
Words
where
are
you
now?

Doubt and Kindness

So gentle were the words she spoke,
so graceful were her ways,
that she scared me with her kindness
and I hid for many days.

And when at last I did return,
I found, to my surprise,
her manner was abrasive
and doubt clouded her eyes.

TV Versus Me

"The days of the old bump and grind are over,"
said the dumb blonde to the exotic dancer as
their two tanned, hard-lined cowboy companions
listened and waited for a chance to unleash
a winter of pent-up passion.
But, they were all on the TV
and television isn't like real life.
The world is full of bumps and grinds;
especially in the night, alone
when turning on your pillow,
loosing a day's worth
of pent up disappointment
into memories.

Maybe

Maybe if one and one
(like you and me)
cannot be one,
or even one two-gether;
maybe then, if Spring fails
to melt the Winter's ice,
we can, at least, learn again
to do used-to-bes
without the Foralways
and maybe then, one and one
can still be more than two.

Closing Night

Goodnight
the darkness closes in
as the theater spills its patrons
into the street.
The last act is finished,
the curtain is down,
no fanfare,
no standing ovation,
mild applause.
The reviews, save the one
from the underground rag,
were all bad.

The players will look
for new work in the morning.
The theater will house
a new playwright's child.

I leave meekly out the stage entrance
into the alley—
always the alley—
overflowing garbage cans,
stray cats,
stench of vomit.

You join the crowd,
push your way out into the street,
with its bright lights, laughter

smell of hot pretzels,
carnival air.

The crowd moves past the alley
where my unnoticed shadow climbs
a fire escape to a small
cluttered room
to study far into the morning,
reviewing the mistakes
of my past performance,
practicing my new lines.

I Stood There

I stood there
holding you,
staring into eyes
alive with the future,
wondering
how in the world
would I ever
convince you/I/we/ this
is all for real
and not about
to go away when
someone flicks off the projector
and sweeps the popcorn
from beneath the seats.

(Your face in silhouette
   against the softening sky
      says this is so good, so real
        so right.)

Taking the Trouble

I walked to your
back door last night
and saw two legs standing
where mine might have been.
I panicked, stepped backwards
down the stoop steps,
retreated to the side of the house
and plotted.
Then I knocked on your door.
"Are you coming?" I asked.
You were confused, drunk,
shaken by his visit—
but smiling.
"How are you?" I asked his beard.
"I'm coming from behind my mask,"
he said. "My ass," I thought.
You said you'd be along shortly.
I waited through the long night
for your scream
or a slamming door.

Tellin' Ruth Ellen

Ruth Ellen, I'm tellin'
you this is great.
no time for fear,
don't hesitate.
You gave me a sign,
I gave you a kiss,
I was afraid to believe
it could be like this.

Ruth Ellen, I'm tellin'
you I'm in love.
There, I've said it,
is that enough?
You gave me a kiss,
we fell to the ground,
bodies pressed, passion pulsing,
stars swirling around.

Ruth Ellen, I'm tellin'
you what I want
is to freeze time.
Don't say we can't.
You gave me believe,
I opened my heart.
If there's an end to this tale
then let's stretch the start.

Ruth Ellen, I'm tellin'
you I feel light,

David Allen

sure I could fly
if the wind is right.
You gave me all this,
a smile in your eye.
I take it to treasure, no
pretending, no lies.

Fool

A fool was I who thought
life could be lived alone,
a hermit crab,
empty while full of myself.
A fool was I who thought
life could be lived without love;
love is life's blood,
and empty, bloodless
we stand alone,
too numb to realize
we should lie down and die.
A fool was I who thought
life could be lived alone,
full of myself.
A fool was I who thought
that I was alive,
now that her touch,
her kiss, her look
have transfused color into
gray, unyielding flesh.
Resurrected, I stand
beside her and say,
"Yes, this is life!"

As My Love Lay Declining

As my love is tied
against the ropes,
the disease delivering
jarring jabs,
but no knockout blows,
I watch outside the ring
observing the slow
destruction of the body
for which I ache.
I want to embrace her,
but she is in the ring
with disease.
The referee, Death,
ignores the head butting
and blows beneath the belt.
I want to jump into the ring,
to stand in for her,
take it on the chin.
But the best I can do
is wait in her corner
with a bucket of fear
for her to spit in
and a towel of love
to wipe away
the sweat
and tears
and blood.

In My Mind

In my mind
I am always with you.
In my mind
you are always well.

In my mind
my kisses do not hurt you.
In my mind
there isn't any hell.

In my mind
your hair is turning darker,
you bruises have all faded,
your life is turning 'round.

In my mind
you've regained your balance,
you sleep uninterrupted,
your restraints are all unbound.

In my mind
there are no muscle spasms.
In my mind
the phantom bees have lost their sting.

In my mind
we have spanned the chasms.
In my mind
pain is not a daily thing.

In my mind
you have regained your color,
you awaken with a smile,
you've found the will to carry on.

In my mind
yesterday's but a nightmare,
a memory that is fading
in the bright glow of a new dawn.

In my mind
love is flowing freely,
unencumbered by this illness
that lurks around each corner
threatening this fragile peace.

In my mind
I imagine you are healthy
and then I cry in dark frustration
when I reluctantly remember—
it's all just in my mind.

(more)

As I was preparing the text for this second printing, I quietly celebrated my 60th birthday. I was going to ignore it until I read somewhere that 60 is the new 50—or even 40.

Then Ruth Ellen told me she doesn't think I'll ever grow up!

So, here's some birthday poems.

David Allen

TWO THIRDS

Two thirds of my life is over
And I'm not sure what I have done
Two-thirds of my life is over
And I feel like I just begun
When I look in the bathroom mirror
I don't like what I see
When I stare at my face in the morning
I want to scream, "This can't be me!"
But then I look in the eyes of my lover
And I kiss the lips of my muse
And it's then that I discover
I'm not old, I'm just confused.

DECADES FROM NOW

The newsman still likes to type
And read aloud the words he writes
Even though nobody sees them
The papers shut down long ago.

He writes about the things he's seen
Characters who shaped his dreams
And the novel where he revived them
But he left the book unfinished long ago
And he falls asleep as his beer loses its foam.

Let us go to our house on the island
On the shore of the East China Sea
Long ago I used to be a writer
And Ruth Ellen remembers that for me.

Grandkids crawling across the floor
The dog is running out the door
The poet's not far behind him
Ball in his hand for the dog to chase.

The tropic sun is burning bright
As he throws the ball with all his might
Last night's troubled sleep behind him
And for an instant it's like he never aged
The ball arcing in the air is his new poem.

(To be continued)